What Happens When I Hiccup?

By Daisy Allyn

Gareth Stevens
Publishing

Please visit our website, www.garethstevens.com. For a free color catalog of all our high-quality books, call toll free 1-800-542-2595 or fax 1-877-542-2596.

Library of Congress Cataloging-in-Publication Data

Allyn, Daisy
What happens when I hiccup? / Daisy Allyn.
  p. cm. — (My body does strange stuff)
Includes index.
ISBN 978-1-4339-9339-8 (pbk.)
ISBN 978-1-4339-9340-4 (6-pack)
ISBN 978-1-4339-9338-1 (library binding)
1. Hiccups —Juvenile literature. 2. Reflexes — Juvenile literature. 3. Reflexes. I.Title
QP372.A443 2014
612.74—d23

Published in 2014 by
Gareth Stevens Publishing
111 East 14th Street, Suite 349
New York, NY 10003

Designer: Michael J. Flynn
Editor: Greg Roza

Photo credits: Cover, p. 1 Blend Images/Shutterstock.com; p. 5 DigitalFabiani/Shutterstock.com; p. 7 CLIPAREA|Custom media/Shutterstock.com; p. 9 udaix/Shutterstock.com; p. 11 konstantynov/Shutterstock.com; p. 13 Shutterstock.com; p. 15 Melanie DeFazio/Shutterstock.com; p. 17 holbox/Shutterstock.com; p. 19 Leah-Anne Thompson.

Printed in the United States of America

CPSIA compliance information: Batch #CS13GS: For further information contact Gareth Stevens, New York, New York at 1-800-542-2595.

Contents

Boldface words appear in the glossary.

How Annoying!

A hiccup is a short breath of air. The breath ends suddenly, which causes the "hic" sound we make when hiccuping. Hiccups usually last for just a few minutes. Sometimes they can last a lot longer. Hiccups can be very **annoying**!

5

Hic!

When we breathe, air passes in through the nose or mouth. The air passes a flap called the epiglottis, down through a tube called the trachea (TRAY-kee-uh), and into the lungs. When we hiccup, the epiglottis closes quickly, causing the "hic" sound.

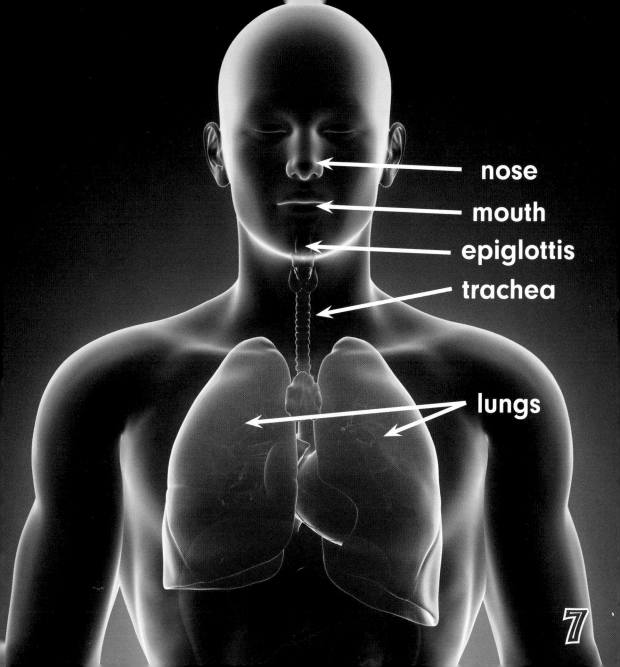

nose

mouth

epiglottis

trachea

lungs

7

Breathing In

The diaphragm (DY-uh-fram) is a large **muscle** below the lungs. It helps us breathe. The diaphragm moves down when we breathe in. It moves up when we breathe out. The diaphragm is what causes us to breathe in very quickly when we hiccup.

breathe in

breathe out

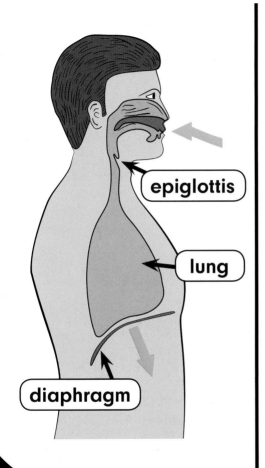

epiglottis

lung

diaphragm

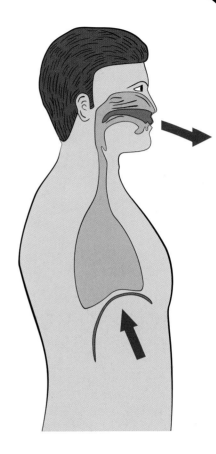

Like the rest of the body, the diaphragm has **nerves** in it. Some things can bother the diaphragm's nerves. The result is a spasm, or a sudden, uncontrolled movement. This causes us to breathe in quickly during a hiccup.

11

I'm So Full!

Perhaps the most common cause of hiccups is eating or drinking too much. A full stomach pushes on the diaphragm. This can bother the nerves of the diaphragm and cause it to have spasms. Spicy food is known to cause hiccups, too.

13

Hot and Cold

A quick change in temperature inside the stomach can cause hiccups. For example, this can happen when someone drinks a cup of hot chocolate and then drinks a cold glass of water right after.

How You Feel

Sometimes our feelings can cause hiccups, too. This can happen when you're feeling **stress**, such as when you're studying for an important test. A sudden shock, such as a loud noise, can cause hiccups. **Excitement** can cause hiccups, too.

Boo!

There's no sure way to stop hiccups, but some things may work. Some people hold their breath or breathe into a paper bag. Some people eat a spoonful of sugar or honey. Other people think a sudden noise scares the hiccups away!

19

I Can't Stop!

Bad cases of hiccups can last hours, days, and even weeks. The longest case of hiccups lasted 68 years! Long-lasting hiccups are usually a sign of some other illness. If your hiccups last longer than 2 days, you should see a doctor.

21

Glossary

annoying: having to do with something that bothers you or makes you a little mad

excitement: having strong or lively feelings about something

muscle: one of the parts of the body that allow movement

nerve: a part of the body that sends messages to the brain and allows us to feel things

stress: a state of concern, worry, or feeling nervous

For More Information

Books

Durant, Penny. *Sniffles, Sneezes, Hiccups, and Coughs.* New York, NY: DK Publishing, 2005.

Fromer, Liza, and Francine Gerstein, MD. *My Noisy Body.* Plattsburgh, NY: Tundra Books, 2011.

Websites

KidsHealth
kidshealth.org/kid
Find more information about hiccuping and many other health topics.

13 Techniques to Cure the Hiccups
health.howstuffworks.com/wellness/natural-medicine/ home-remedies/13-techniques-to-cure-the-hiccups.htm
Learn more about hiccups and the science behind some of the more popular cures.

Index